I'm a little mermaid
hiding in the sea,

2 whopping whales!

Can you find me?

I'm a little mermaid
hiding in the sea,

3 snapping sharks!

Can you find me?

I'm a little mermaid
hiding in the sea,

I'm a little mermaid
hiding in the sea,

5
dancing dolphins!

Can you find me?

I'm a little mermaid
hiding in the sea,

6 sparkling **starfish!** Can you find me?

1
2
3
4
5
6

I'm a little mermaid
hiding in the sea,

7

tubby turtles!

Can you find me?

1
2
3
4
5
6
7

I'm a little mermaid
hiding in the sea,

I'm a little mermaid
hiding in the sea,

9 clawing crabs!

Can you find me?

1
2
3
4
5
6
7
8
9

I'm a little mermaid
hiding in the sea,

10 **flashy fish!** Can you find me?

1
2
3
4
5
6
7
8
9
10

I'm a little mermaid
swimming in the sea,